Badri Seshadri

Life
Badri Seshadri ©

First Edition: January 2008
80 Pages
Printed in India.

ISBN 978-81-8368-651-8
Pro-ya-en - 7

Prodigy Books
177/103, First Floor, Ambal's Building
Lloyds Road, Royapettah, Chennai 600 014.
Ph: +91-44-4200-9603
Email: support@nhm.in
Website: www.nhm.in

Prodigy Books is an imprint of New Horizon Media Pvt. Ltd.

1. Introduction

You wake up every morning to the voice of your dear mother. At school, you like your teachers and you love your friends. After a great day, you are back home. You run and hug your father who has come back from work. You play with your brother and sister and your pet dog. After finishing your homework and watching the antics of Tom and Jerry, and a tasty dinner with your family, it's time for bed. Everything is going fine and you are happy.

Life is great.

The next morning, you hear the old man in the next house is dead. Everybody is sad.

You run to your mother and she says—everyone born on this earth has to die one day. Isn't that scary?

So there are births and deaths happening always.

Now stop for a moment and ask yourself—was it always like this? Was there life always on this earth? When did life start on our earth?

*

In this book, we try to understand how life forms might have come about in the earth, through a scientific process.

Since life forms need a place to live, we will first try to understand how the universe in which the life forms live, might have come about.

2. Origin of the universe

Scientists have estimated that the universe we live in today was formed roughly 13.7 billion years ago.

All the matter in the universe, including that in living organisms and non-living organisms was packed into a single ball of plasma, not larger than the palm of your hand. The pressure was just too much to handle and this ball exploded.

After the explosion, the matter contained in the ball started expanding. Sub-atomic particles known as electrons, protons and neutrons were created.

Celestial bodies known as stars were formed. The stars contained electrons and protons. Under extreme pressure and heat, a process called nuclear fusion started. This resulted in the creation of elements such as Hydrogen and Helium.

Continuing nuclear fusion resulted in further new elements such as Lithium, Boron, Beryllium, Carbon, Nitrogen, Oxygen and many more.

Some of the pieces of the stars containing these elements burst off and started cooling. They later settled down as planets.

Our earth is one such planet.

Stars gathered together to form galaxies. There are several galaxies in the universe. Our galaxy is known as the Milky Way galaxy. Our sun is only one of the several billions of stars in our galaxy.

All stars radiate heat and light, because of the nuclear fusion happening in their cores. It is because of this reason that our sun is extremely hot and sends light and heat towards our earth.

Heavy objects attract one another by a force called gravity. Smaller objects start circling around the heavier objects.

Thus, eight planets including our earth circle the sun. Our earth has its own little satellite called the Moon. The Moon on its own does not possess any energy to radiate light. It picks up light from the sun and reflects the light back to the earth.

All heavenly objects such as the planets including our earth, the moon, the sun and various stars are spherical in shape.

The earth rotates on its own axis. The portion of our spherical earth facing the sun is bright and that period is called a day. The portion that does not see the sun experiences night. It takes about 24 hours for day and night to repeat again. That is the same time taken for the earth to complete one rotation about its axis.

The earth circles the sun over a period of 365 earth days (365 days of 24 hours each). This process keeps repeating forever.

*

Our earth is in an ideal position. It is not too far from the sun, nor too near. Hence it is not too hot, nor too cold. It has an excellent protective shield called the atmosphere which keeps away harmful radiation from the sun. This shield allows just the right amount of heat and light to pass through to the surface of the earth.

The temperature on the surface of the earth is ideal for life to thrive. Sunlight is essential for plants to create their food.

The earth is blessed with many basic elements, 92 of which occur naturally. Of this, the element Carbon is the most important to support life. All living beings are made of Carbon compounds.

The atmosphere consists of the elements Oxygen and Nitrogen. Hydrogen is available in plenty in the form of water, which is a compound made up of Hydrogen and Oxygen.

All animals and plants are mainly made up of the above four elements. In the human body, for example, Oxygen is 65% by weight, Carbon 18%, Hydrogen 10% and Nitrogen 3%. All the other elements form the remaining 4%.

For different animals and plants, the composition may be slightly different. But effectively, it is the same four elements that form the bulk of animal and plant bodies.

*

Let us now examine what life is and how it has been viewed historically.

3. Life as we knew it in the earlier days

Life has always been a mystery, though humans could always distinguish between plants and animals. Plants did not move around. They were mostly rooted to the ground. Animals, insects and birds moved around. They walked, ran, crawled or flew.

Humans recognised that plants produced food which could be picked up for human consumption. Some plants were also helpful as medicines. They could cure diseases that attacked human beings.

But man had to be careful. Some plants produced poisonous substances sometimes leading to death.

Animals and birds were also food for humans, who had to run and catch animals or shoot down birds with arrows.

Some animals were quite dangerous. They in turn, hunted humans. Lions, tigers and other wild animals attacked unarmed humans.

Growing plants

One of the earliest things humans understood was to learn to grow plants they wanted. Most plants required good soil. The seed of the plant needed to be planted in the soil. It needed water. Slowly the seed germinated and formed roots and shoots. This plant needed sufficient sunlight. Then, it started growing on its own and produced leaves, grains, vegetables and ripe fruits. And humans could eat them all.

Humans identified the right kind of plants. They picked the seeds of these plants and domesticated these plants. Over several generations, seeds were preserved and distributed. There were several varieties of the same plants, but humans chose those that produced either more food or produced food that was tasty.

Rice, wheat and corn are some of the staple food grains used by human beings as food. Besides foodgrains, vegetables and fruits from several plants were used as food. Several hundred medicinal plants were also used by different societies.

In addition, several plants were grown for their beauty. Their flowers were colourful and bright.

Some plants were grown for the food they produced—not for human consumption, but for the consumption of animals domesticated by humans.

<u>Domesticating animals and birds</u>

Humans identified specific breeds of animals they wanted to eat and started domesticating them. The animals were brought up in captivity. They learnt not to attack their human owners.

The opposite of a domestic animal is a wild animal. A wild animal either runs away from humans or attacks humans.

The cow and sheep are the most well known domesticated animals. They provide milk and meat. They feed on grass and leaves.

Bulls and donkeys were domesticated and made to pull carts filled with goods.

Horses were domesticated as war-time animals, to carry the soldiers who fought wars.

Even the large elephants were domesticated to carry kings, fight wars and pull heavy objects.

Trained pigeons were used for sending written messages from one place to another.

Parrots and other pet birds were kept as companions by humans.

Chicken, duck and other fowl were grown for food.

<u>Classification and study</u>

We will use the term 'animals' from here on to denote all living organisms that are not plants. So birds, fish and insects (and human beings too) will come under the term animals.

More than 2000 years ago, Aristotle, a great Greek philosopher, studied animals and plants. He classified animals based on how they reproduced.

Some animals reproduced by laying eggs, which then hatched into offspring. Some animals directly gave birth to their offspring in the full and final form. Some animals laid eggs, which in turn went through a few other stages before the final young ones came into being.

In most societies, plants and animals were known by a common name, which varied from one language to another.

An attempt was made starting from the 16th century to classify them in Latin, the language of education across Europe.

The system in use now was developed by the Swedish biologist Carolus Linnaeus who lived between 1707 and 1778 AD.

He divided groups of plants and animals into detailed classifications containing class, order, genus, species and variety. A class contained several orders. Each order in turn had several genuses and each genus contained several species.

A specific plant or animal was referred to by its genus and species. Thus, the common cockroach we see is called Periplanata Americana. 'Periplanata' is its genus. 'Americana' is the species.

Cockroaches occupy a class known as Insecta, which is the Latin word for insects. Their order is called Blattodea. Under the cockroach family's order Blattodea, there are several genuses and several species.

Since the time of Linnaeus, every known plant and animal has been carefully studied and a name given to each one of them. Each has been slotted into some class, some order, some genus and some species.

This classification and organisation is known as Taxonomy.

Let us now turn our attention to what we actually mean by the term life.

<u>Life</u>

We humans are considered alive, or full of life, when we move around. We consume food to generate the required energy to move. We grow in size from the time we are born. When we stop eating for a short time, we lose the energy to move. We feel hunger. If we do not take food for a long time, our internal organs fail and we die.

If you look at other animals, they too behave like humans. They move around. They consume food to get energy.

They grow up from the time they are born.

In addition, all animals including humans reproduce. They produce offspring which look more or less similar to their parents.

So anything that moves, reproduces and consumes food to sustain itself can be considered to have life.

We have so far not observed any animal that can live forever. All animals have a fixed lifetime. It could be only a few minutes or it could be 100 years. It could be anything in between. Some species of animals can live for more than 100 years. The Galapagos tortoise has a life span of over 200 years!

<u>What about plants?</u>

Plants do not move. But they do grow.

They do not seem to consume any food in the manner animals do. On closer observation, we find that they create their own food (more of this later), and consume the food they have themselves created. They need water, air and sunlight to create their food.

Plants reproduce. Similar looking small plants grow from the seeds of their mother plants.

Plants die. They wither away naturally or get eaten by animals.

In this sense, even without moving around, plants should be treated as life forms.

Is that all? Let us first take a more detailed look at the life forms we see all around us.

4. Plants

We see a variety of plants around us. Scientists estimate that there could be more than 300, 000 different species of plants around us.

The normal plants we see around us have roots and shoots. While roots are hidden deep in the soil, shoots are above the soil. Shoots have branches and sub-branches. Leaves grow on these branches. Flowers grow on the branches. Flowers turn into vegetables. Vegetables ripen to fruits. These fruits contain seeds.

And planting these seeds in the soil results in them germinating, and growing roots and shoots. The whole process as detailed above continues.

However, not all plants fit into the above model. There are variations.

Plants are largely of four types, based on their behaviour.

(a) Moss

The soft, mat-like growth in moist and damp conditions is called moss. We often see them in ponds and in poorly kept bathrooms in houses. They also grow at the base of other large trees. They are between 1 to 10 centimetres tall in size. They do not produce any flowers or seeds.

They have thin stems and thinner leaves on the stem. They do not have well defined roots.

There are around 10,000 species in this category. Botanically, they are known as Bryophyta.

(b) Fern

Ferns have well defined stems and leaves. They also have roots. However they do not have flowers and seeds.

They grow in a variety of climates. They are found in deserts, mountains and plains.

Botanically, they are known as Pteridophyta. There are over 20,000 different species in this category.

(c) Conifers

Conifers are tall trees with branches, roots and leaves. The leaves are like needles.

These trees do not produce flowers. However, they do form seeds. The seeds are packed together in cones. These seeds spread and create new plants of the species.

Botanically, they are known as Pinophyta. There are only a few hundred known species in this category.

(d) Flowering Plants

These are the most common type of plants we know and see everyday.

There are well defined roots and shoots. The stem consists of several branches. The branches carry leaves and flowers. Flowers become seed-bearing fruits.

Botanically, they are known as Magnoliophyta. This group has the largest number of species amongst plants.

Flowering plants range from small to large. They are in the form of herbs, shrubs and large trees. They also occur as creepers, without a firm stem. They grow tall upwards or grow to spread over a large area.

Reproduction

All the four types of plants mentioned above reproduce in a more or less similar manner.

Mosses are of two types: male and female. The males release sperms and the females release eggs which are specialised cells. These cells meet each other to create fertilised eggs called zygotes. This zygote floats, moves out and grows into another moss.

In the case of ferns, there is no male or female tree. The same tree produces male cells known as sperms and female cells known as eggs. The egg remains attached to the tree while the sperm floats in air. Sperm cells reach the egg cells of the same plant or another plant, fertilise the eggs and create zygotes.

The zygotes float in air, fall down to the soil, take root and grow.

In case of conifers, each tree generates male cones and female cones. Male cones are filled with male cells or sperms in the form of pollen. Female cones contain female egg cells. Pollen flies in the air and reaches the eggs, fertilises them and creates zygotes.

The zygotes stay in the female cone and mature. There may be some unfertilised eggs as well in the female cone. The fertilised and mature zygotes become seeds. They fall down and grow, or in some cases, they get eaten by birds which drop them along with their droppings. The dropped seeds may then grow into a tree.

Flowering plants have a well-developed reproduction mechanism. Each tree starts producing brightly coloured and scented flowers. Each plant in this category produces different looking flowers.

Every flower consists of both pollen (male sperm) and female eggs.

Flowers have developed a complex method to spread their pollen. Several flowers produce sweet nectar (what we know as honey). Insects and small birds feed on this nectar. At this time, the pollen in the flowers sticks to the bodies of the insects or the birds. When the birds go to another flower, the pollen gets inside the flower, reach the ovary and fertilise the eggs.

Once the pollen fertilises the egg, a vegetable like structure is formed, in which the fertilised seeds are hidden.

Now, the seeds have to be distributed. This is done by animals and birds which eat the fruits and spread the seeds in the process.

*

The method of reproduction through sperm and eggs is known as sexual reproduction.

However, several plants also reproduce through asexual method. That is, there will not be any sperm or eggs. When a part of the stem of some plants (like the commonly available drumstick plant) are cut and planted in the soil, they start growing into a new tree. In some cases the tuber (which is the underground part of the stem) can be taken and replanted. This will grow into another plant. Examples are potato, beetroot, carrot, etc.

However, the more common form of reproduction in plants is sexual reproduction.

<u>Producing food</u>

Plants have the ability to create their own food.

This is done through a brilliant process in their leaves. All plants have a special chemical in their leaves known as chlorophyll. This is a green coloured pigment. That is why leaves are green in colour.

Chlorophyll combines carbon dioxide and water in the presence of sunlight and converts them into a sugary compound called glucose. In addition to creating glucose, this process also releases plenty of oxygen into the atmosphere. This process is known as photosynthesis.

Part of the glucose thus created is consumed by the plant. The rest of the glucose is moved to other parts where it is converted into starch in the form of vegetables and fruits. These, in turn, are consumed by animals.

Without plants producing glucose, other life forms cannot exist. A continuous release of oxygen into the atmosphere is also important as animals require oxygen for breathing.

Plant-like life forms

Some life forms are closely related to plants but differ from them in certain features.

Mushroom, fungus and toadstool are some of the life forms which do not produce their own food. They do not possess chlorophyll. They convert bio-waste into food for themselves. They grow on leftover food or wood waste or bio-garbage waste. Some of them grow on living in trees as parasites and suck the energy out of the living tree.

While some mushroom species are edible, there are other poisonous mushroom varieties too.

Algae are also not considered as plants even though most algae make food through photosynthesis. And then, there are those varieties which take food from external sources.

Though plants produce their own food from carbon dioxide and sunlight, there are some plants that swallow little insects and animals! These plants kill animals not for their energy, but for their nutrients.

In addition, these plants do make their own food using chlorophyll as usual. But besides food, they also need minerals and nutrients. Normally, plants take such nutrients from the soil. When the soil is depleted, what can these plants do?

These plants have developed very smart trapping methods. When an insect or a small bird sits on their flowers, the flowers suddenly close, trapping the insect or the bird inside and suck its juices out.

*

By now we have a reasonable idea of the plant kingdom. Let us now take a look at the animal kingdom.

5. Animals

The animal kingdom is much bigger than the plant kingdom. It is estimated that there are more than one million species of animals!

Unlike plants, animals cannot make their own food. They either eat plants or other animals to get their energy.

But animals have one important ability that plants do not have. When an enemy approaches, animals can run or fly away. A plant, on the other hand, is rooted where it is.

Animals are largely divided into two major groups: those with vertebrae or backbones, and those without backbones, known as invertebrates.

Invertebrates

Of all animal varieties, invertebrates form the bulk. They live across a variety of habitats—in water, over land, under the ground and as parasites in human and other animal bodies.

They can be classified under the following categories:

(a) Sponges

Sponges are water animals. They live mostly in seawater. Animals which live in seawater are known as marine lifeforms.

These are the simplest animals we can see with our naked eye. They have no internal organs, no muscles or nerves. They swallow seawater along with sea organisms for food and then filter out the water alone. The food stays inside and gets digested.

Zoologically, they are known as Porifera.

Sponges reproduce through two methods. They split into two parts and each part continues to grow as separate lives. This is asexual reproduction.

Alternately, they also produce male cells (sperm) and female cells (eggs). These cells float in the water, fertilise and form zygotes. The zygote grows into offspring sponges. This is sexual reproduction.

(b) Jelly fish and Coral

These are also water-based animals. They are mostly marine animals but some forms exist in freshwater as well.

In these animals, we see the beginning of the development of internal organs. They have a stomach. Many of them have tentacles. They grab their prey and start digesting them outside their stomach by applying some enzymes on their prey. The semi-digested food is taken into the stomach and fully digested.

Jelly fish, sea anemones, coral and several other similar species belong to this category.

Zoologically, they are split into two groups: Cnidaria and Ctenophora.

They reproduce through both sexual and asexual methods. In some species, the animal generates a 'bud'. This bud falls off and gives birth to a new animal. In other species, sperm and eggs are created and expelled into the water. They fertilise and create baby animals.

(c) Parasitic worms

These are worms which live only within a host body. The hosts will be other animals including humans. They live in the intestinal tracts of their hosts. They eat the food available inside intestines and in the process affect the hosts.

They have a tubular body, a well defined head end and a rear end. They consume their food through a mouth-like opening.

They reproduce sexually. However, the same worms have both male and female sexual organs. Such animals are known as hermaphrodites.

Hermaphrodites behave as either male or female. When the sperm fertilises the egg, the resultant fertilised egg creates a larva. The larva then becomes the complete baby worm.

Zoologically, they are known as Helminthes.

These worms cannot live on their own. They pass on from host to host at various stages, either as an egg or larva or as fully grown adult worms.

(d) Worms

Some worms, leeches and other similar species live in an external environment unlike parasitic worms.

In addition to a head and a mouth, they have an opening for excretion called the anus. They have a very basic blood circulation system. Through pores all over their body, they absorb oxygen from the surroundings directly into their blood.

Zoologically they are called Annelida. Some annelids reproduce asexually. They split into two with each part living separately.

Other annelids reproduce sexually. Several of them are hermaphrodites, as in the case of parasitic worms.

However, several annelid species show distinct male and female animals. They perform separate functions. The male animal produces sperm while the female animal produces eggs.

In the case of annelids, unlike the previous cases, a male and female reproduce by coming into contact with each other. The male releases the sperm inside the body of the female, where the eggs are fertilised.

(e) Insects

This is the largest category of animals under invertebrates. It covers all kinds of insects, bugs, bees, ants, crabs and so on.

The most distinctive feature of these species is well defined legs with joints in the legs. They have a hard body shell. Several species have wings and can fly. Others can only crawl.

They have a blood circulation system. There is also a basic respiratory system in them.

All species here reproduce only sexually. They have distinct male and female members in each species.

(f) Squid, Snail, Octopus, etc.

Known zoologically as Mollusca, this division consists of mostly marine animals.

They have a reasonably developed nervous system, in addition to a digestive system, a blood circulatory system and a respiratory system.

They have distinct male and female animals and reproduce sexually.

(g) Star fish and Shell fish

These are marine animals, known zoologically as Echinodermata.

Some species in this division reproduce asexually. However, the predominant mode is sexual reproduction.

Vertebrates

Vertebrates are animals that contain a well developed skeletal system with a backbone. In addition, they have:

- A digestive system with a mouth, an intestinal portion where food gets digested and an anus through which waste is sent out.

- A blood circulatory system, where the blood carries energy and nutrients across the body, along with a heart used for pumping blood.

- A central nervous system consisting of nerves for sending signals to various parts of the body and a brain that controls the nervous system.

- A respiratory system for absorbing oxygen from the air with gills or lungs.

Vertebrates are broadly classified into five major categories.

1. Reptiles, 2. Amphibians, 3. Fish, 4. Birds, 5. Mammals

Lizards and snakes belong to the reptile family. Frogs and crocodiles are amphibians. We see a few thousand fish and bird varieties regularly. Mammals consist of all four-legged animals (including humans) which give birth to their young ones directly and feed them with milk secreted in the mother.

Whales and dolphins, though living under water, are mammals. But all other mammals live on land.

Birds have well developed wings and they fly. Some birds like the ostrich, kiwi and emu, have lost the ability to fly. Some reptiles too can fly.

All vertebrates reproduce sexually, with distinct male and female animals in each species. The male and female come into contact with each other, resulting in the male transferring sperm into the female body, where fertilisation takes place.

Except for mammals, all the others lay fertilised eggs. These eggs hatch into offspring.

In the case of mammals, the fertilised egg stays inside an internal organ known as the uterus. The entire baby is formed inside the body of the female animal. The fully grown baby animal comes out of the mother.

Some mammals can give birth to several offspring in a single instance. Humans usually give birth to only one offspring at a time, though we know twins and triplets.

*

In the case of plants, their most important feature was the ability to produce their own food. In the case of animals, the equivalent feature is the ability to find their food from plant or animal sources.

The success of an individual animal depends on its ability to find food for itself and find a mate with which it can produce offspring. The animal needs energy to grow and produce offspring.

Several animals live entirely on food from plants. They are known as herbivores. Their organs are developed to digest plant food. They have internal organs in their bodies to process plant food. The cow, deer and elephant are herbivores.

Some animals survive by eating the flesh of other animals. They are known as carnivores. So their body parts and digestive system can only handle such food.

Certain animals eat both plants and animals. Such animals are known as omnivores.

*

Just as plants use chlorophyll to convert carbon dioxide and water into glucose, animals have their own systems to convert the complex food they eat, into simple glucose. This is done in the digestive system.

Animals get their energy, when glucose is burnt in the body in the presence of oxygen. This is why animals need oxygen. They either absorb oxygen from air through their skin or use their lungs to extract oxygen from air. Sea animals use oxygen dissolved in water for this purpose. Oxygen is vital for generating energy inside an animal's body.

When an animal does not get oxygen, it stops living.

*

Let us revisit plants and animals again later. But before that, let's take a look at some living forms we have not seen so far.

6. Microscope and Microbes

Lenses are glass pieces ground in a particular shape. They help to magnify objects. If you look at objects through a convexly ground lens, the objects look much bigger than they are.

Objects which are not normally visible to human eyes can be seen through convex lenses.

Lenses can be used to see objects which are far away and cannot be seen by the naked eye. An instrument with such lenses is called a telescope. When the same lenses are used to see small objects, we call the instrument a microscope.

Microscopes and telescopes were first made in the 17th century. Telescopes made the study of celestial bodies and the nature of the universe clearer. Likewise, microscopes allowed scientists to learn about an amazing new world of life.

The Netherlands was the centre of lens-making.

Antonie van Leeuwenhoek was born in Netherlands in 1632. He learnt to make excellent lenses. A clothes merchant, he used his microscope to judge the quality of the clothes he was buying and selling. Soon, he started using the microscope to look at the natural world.

When he examined a drop of lake water through his microscope, he could see several small objects moving around. These objects were also multiplying. It became clear to Leeuwenhoek that they were life forms.

That is how he discovered single-celled life forms.

Thus was born a new field known as microbiology.

The importance of microbes was not that well known until the 19th century. Until then, medical practitioners did not know why suddenly some people (and animals) were affected by mysterious diseases. Doctors came up with some medicines which sometimes helped, sometimes did not.

People died in large numbers when affected by such mysterious diseases as plague and pox, with no remedy in sight.

Louis Pasteur, a French scientist who lived between 1822 and 1895, proposed the theory that most of the diseases affecting animals were caused by microbes known as germs.

Scientists could link different human and animal diseases to the microbes causing such diseases.

These microbes are largely divided into single-celled organisms called bacteria and protozoa.

Cell

A cell is the basic building block of all life forms. Micro-organisms possess only one cell.

A cell is surrounded by a wall containing a liquid protein. In some single-celled life forms, the cell possesses a nucleus—an inner portion covered by a membrane. Such microbes are called protozoa.

Other single-celled organisms do not have a well defined nucleus. Instead, the material that should be part of the nucleus floats around freely in the liquid. Such organisms are called bacteria.

All animals and plants have millions of cells. All their cells have a nucleus in them.

In a multi-celled life form, a cell is a self-contained unit. It absorbs nutrients. It can convert the nutrients into energy. The cell is a chemical factory. All the chemicals required for animals or plants are created inside their cells.

In single-celled organisms, reproduction happens through cell replication.

In multi-celled organisms like plants too, growth occurs through cell replication. The root grows by replication of existing root cells and the stem grows by replication of existing stem cells.

How do microbes affect animals and plants?

Single-celled microbes attack plants and animals by entering their bodies. Once inside, each microbe attacks one specific cell, cuts the cell wall and enters. Once inside the cell, the microbe absorbs the nutrients in the cell for its own purpose, thereby affecting the normal functioning of the host plant or animal. If this is left unchecked, the animal or plant becomes weak and develops a disease.

Plants and animals have developed their own defence systems against microbes. They send what are called antibodies which attack invading microbes. As microbes have superior (chemical) weapons to handle antibodies, multi-cellular life forms are not always successful in fighting microbes. When the microbes win the battle, the host organism dies.

Not all microbes are bad. Animals have several parasitic microbes living in their digestive tract which help in breaking up undigested food. Some microbes help in recycling bio-waste in the world. Microbes can even break up oil slicks formed in the ocean when crude oil spills into the ocean. You may have heard that plastics cause pollution and they are bad for the environment. Certain varieties of microbes can eat up plastics and thus cut down pollution.

Without microbes, grape juice will not become wine and milk will not become curd or buttermilk or cheese. At the same time, microbes destroy food items such as meat and cooked food exposed to the air for a long time.

<u>Well then, do microbes come under life forms?</u>

Though very primitive, microbes are life forms too. They reproduce. They are mobile. They consume food for their energy.

The microbe's nucleus has a protein which is called Deoxyribonucleic Acid (DNA).

Microbes reproduce by cell-splitting. During reproduction, the nucleus inside the cell is first replicated. Then the cell wall grows inwards and divides the cell into two with the two nuclear chunks on either side. Eventually the cell wall divides the original cell into two and they become two organisms.

Virus

Besides bacteria and protozoa, a new set of microbes have also been observed. They are called viruses. Like a bacterium, a virus is also a single-celled organism. A virus cell does not have a nucleus in it. Its nuclear material is not DNA but a chemical called RNA—Ribo Nucleic Acid.

A virus is normally not considered a life form because of the manner of its reproduction.

Unlike a bacterium, a virus does not split itself into two to reproduce. Instead, it attacks a host animal and takes over the cell of the host animal or plant. Once inside the host, the virus stops the functioning of the host cell.

We have seen that the host cell is a chemical factory producing some protein or chemical compound. The virus changes the production plan of the host cell and forces the host cell instead to produce copies of the virus's RNA. The RNA in turn becomes new viruses.

Thus, a virus does not truly reproduce in the manner in which other life forms reproduce, but it does have the ability to create copies of itself through other life forms.

Antibiotics and Vaccines

In 1928, the biologist Alexander Fleming accidentally discovered ways of killing a bacterium.

It was known since the time of Pasteur that microbes were causing diseases, but, no medicines were discovered to kill these microbes.

Pasteur had found a method to prevent human beings and animals from being affected by microbes. Pasteur developed a diluted solution containing the microbes, called a vaccine. When a person was injected with this vaccine, the person's body developed antibodies capable of fighting the bacteria.

Vaccines were successfully developed for some diseases, but could not help to fight several diseases. That was when Fleming's accidental discovery happened.

One day Fleming left some bacteria in the open in his laboratory. Next day he found many of them dead. A mould of a certain fungus had formed in that dish which had killed the bacteria.

Fleming identified the mould as Penicillium. However, for several years after this discovery, the substance responsible for killing the bacteria could not be extracted. It was only in 1939 that Penicillin was successfully extracted by Howard Florey and Ernst Chain. Fleming, Florey and Chain were awarded the Nobel Prize in medicine in 1945 for their efforts.

Penicillin has been used successfully to treat several bacterial diseases and it is in use even today. Since then, considerable research has been conducted to create organic chemicals capable of attacking specific bacteria. Such chemicals are known as antibiotics.

Though antibiotics can kill bacteria, they cannot kill viruses. In fact, viruses cannot be killed at all! All we can do is prevent viruses from spreading. This has to be done by the host body by producing the right antibodies. However, vaccines can be produced for several viruses.

Micro-fungus

We already saw about funguses under the plant kingdom. There are several varieties of funguses which cannot be seen by the naked eye. Some fungus varieties are single-celled and can only be seen using a microscope.

Micro-animals

All animals are multi-cellular. However, some multi-cellular animals are so small that they can only be seen by a microscope. Dust mites are classic examples. You can see them only through magnifying glasses. They belong to the Arthropoda division.

We have seen various life forms—the ones that can be seen by our eyes and the ones that cannot be seen.

We now have some understanding of how plants produce food and how animals get their energy.

We have seen that the building block of every life form is a cell. Each cell produces a lot of chemicals from basic materials. And cells have the ability to split and make copies of themselves.

But we have several questions still unanswered.

- How does a cell know what to produce?

- How does a cell know how to produce a particular chemical?

- How do various cells interact with each other in a multi-cellular life form? How do they cooperate with one another?

- Who controls the actions of a multi-cellular organism?

- How does a single fertilised cell become an entire animal or plant with specialised cells for each specific activity?

- How do different members within a given species look different? If you take human beings for example, skin colour, hair colour, height, facial look, etc. are different for each member of the species. How does this happen?

Let us find out the answers to these interesting questions.

7. DNA and genes

With the help of more and more powerful microscopes, scientists could observe what was happening inside the fertilised egg of a multi-cellular organism.

The fertilised egg splits first into two. Then, the two become four, eight, sixteen, thirty-two and so on. Initially, each split cell is identical to the original cell from which it is created.

Slowly, they start regrouping and start changing their shape and function.

In the human embryo, cells regroup and roughly form the shape of a human child. Some cells regroup to form the heart, some create lungs, some form kidneys, the skin, the blood, the bones and so on.

Similarly, the fertilised cell of a dog multiplies to create a dog-shaped embryo and eventually creates a dog.

Something similar happens in plant seeds. The entire blueprint of the grown up plant is contained in a single fertilised seed.

Which portion of the cell has this hidden blueprint?

Further tests revealed that everything was stored in the nucleus. We have already seen that the nucleus of a cell contains a chemical called DNA. It was all in the DNA!

In an animal, every cell—whether it is a blood cell or hair cell or skin cell—has identical DNA. It is the same for plants too. DNA is like a fingerprint. If you take two cells and compare their DNAs and if they are identical, they should have come from the same plant or animal.

The DNAs of animals and plants are distinct. Within a given species too, the DNA of one member is different from that of another member. It is this difference in the DNAs that makes members of a particular species look or behave differently.

DNA is a long polymer made of several simple units known as nucleotides and a few compounds known as nucleobases called cytosine (C), guanine (G), adenine (A) and thymine (T).

These nucleobases C, G, A and T are arranged in different orders to build different DNA for various plants and animals. You change the order of these four compounds, and the result is a different DNA, and hence a different animal or plant.

In these C, G, A and T, the entire information about what proteins are to be produced in which cell, is coded. Each cell produces proteins and other compounds as per the blueprint, within the DNA CGAT sequence.

The DNA structure was determined by James Watson and Francis Crick in 1953 based on X-ray images taken by Rosalind Franklin. Watson and Crick were awarded the Nobel Prize in 1962 for their discovery but Franklin was not. She died before that time.

The study of inheritance of characters from parents is quite old. Gregor Mendel, a Christian priest from Austria, studied pea plants carefully, between 1856 and 1863.

He was breeding several varieties of these plants and studied the quality of the peas. Some had smooth surfaces while some were wrinkled. By isolating such plants, Mendel carefully cross-bred them and observed several interesting facts.

There must be something coded in the parent to control external appearance. This is called a 'gene'. There are two (or more) competing genes controlling the same appearance. For example, if one gene resulted in the peas having a smooth surface, another one made the peas wrinkly.

If a smooth pea plant keeps mating with a similar smooth pea plant, all its child plants will over time produce only smooth peas. A child from this lineage is called purebred.

When a purebred smooth pea plant is mated with a purebred wrinkly pea plant, what will happen to the offspring? Mendel found that the offspring were all producing smooth peas. He could not find any wrinkles at all.

However, when he mated two of the first generation offspring the result was three-fourth smooth peas and one-fourth wrinkly ones.

Mendel proposed that of the two genes controlling smoothness and wrinkles, one is dominant and the other recessive. In each plant, a pair of genes exists, both carrying a certain blueprint for a certain characteristic. However, the dominant gene forces the plant to follow its blueprint. The plant ignores the recessive blueprint.

However, the recessive one does not vanish. It stays inside the plant. It propagates itself during sexual reproduction and reaches its grandchild (second generation).

This theory of genes and how they control the various characteristics of a particular life was well known even before DNA was understood.

In the 20th century, scientists started looking for genes inside DNAs.

The order of C, G, A, T inside DNAs was controlling all aspects of a growing embryo.

How are DNAs themselves formed?

If we take asexual reproduction, the DNA of the child is exactly the same as that of its parent. A parent's body is either split off to become the child or a small spore or bud falls off the parent, which then grows to become the child. In this case, the parent and the child are identical genetically.

However, in the case of sexual reproduction, something else happens.

In a normal cell splitting, an identical copy of the DNA is first formed inside the cell. Then the cell wall grows to

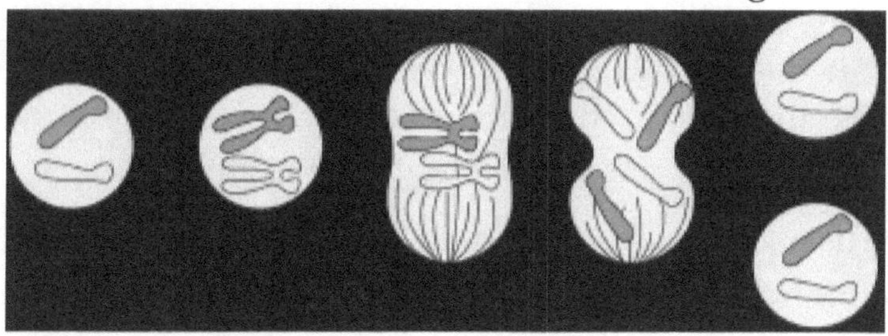

create two identical cells. This process is known as mitosis.

However, during formation of sex cells, DNA material inside normal cells splits into two halves. Each half becomes a separate cell. This process is known as meiosis.

The DNA coil inside cells is called a chromosome. Each cell has an even number of chromosomes. For example, human cells contain 46 chromosomes or 23 pairs of chromosomes. Each pair has competing designs for the parts of the body. Of this, only one design is used.

During sex cell formation, the chromosomes split in such a manner that each sex cell contains only 23 chromosomes. In doing so, care is taken to ensure that competing pairs are split into two halves. It would be a mistake if the two genes controlling the same aspect got into one single sex cell.

During fertilisation of sex cells, sperm and eggs come together. If they are human cells, each cell has 23 chromosomes. When they get together and fertilise, the fertilised egg gets double the chromosomes.

The number of chromosomes in other species varies but they behave in a similar manner. There is a meiotic cell split in the sex cells resulting in halving the number of chromosomes. They double up again during fertilisation.

Similar to other characteristics, the sex of the animal is also determined by genes.

In human beings, sex is determined by chromosomes known as X and Y. If in the offspring, the pair XX resides, the result is a female. XY results in a male.

There are some insect species known as haplo-diploid. Diploid means having a full set of chromosomes. Haploid means having half the chromosomes. In most species, all cells are diploid while sex cells are haploid as we have already seen.

But in the haplo-diploid insects, the females of the species will have normal cells as diploid while the normal cells of males in that species will have only half the chromosomes, or haploid. Fine examples include ants, bees and wasps.

*

What exactly is a gene inside a DNA? Are all genes within a DNA (controlling different aspects) of the same length?

Not really. All genes are packed back to back together inside DNA. Some genes are longer than other genes.

Gene mapping or DNA sequencing is a process by which the specific chunk of DNA that remains together always, is identified. That is one gene. Its chemical sequence is mapped.

If we take the human race, only a handful of genes, various combinations, form the various members of our race. The Human Genome Project estimates that there are about 24,000 different genes in the human DNA strand. There will be variations in each of the genes occupying a particular slot.

Height, weight, colour, skin texture—everything comes from these variations sitting in these 24,000 slots.

It is not that a single gene controls one characteristic completely. One single characteristic can be controlled by more than one gene. Equally, one gene may control more than one feature.

We now have more questions.

- Why are there so many species in the first place?
- Are there species that once existed but are now extinct?
- Have all the species that we see today existed right from day one?
- Are there species that once existed but are now extinct?
- Have all the species that we see today existed right from day one?

Let us try to answer them.

8. Darwin and evolution

Charles Darwin was born on 12 February 1809. He first studied medicine but could not find a job as a doctor. Later, he studied theology to become a priest.

However, he found a job as a naturalist with a ship HMS Beagle, to accompany its captain. Darwin was on board that ship between 24 October 1831 and 2 October 1836. During these five years, the ship sailed from England to South America and returned via New Zealand to England.

During this trip, Darwin found amazing varieties of wildlife and fossils in South America. The fossils proved that so many different animals existed at one time but simply did not exist anymore. The variation in the wildlife he saw made him think about the closeness between several different species.

Though by 1838 Darwin had developed his theory of natural selection and discussed it with a friend in 1844, he was afraid to publish it because he felt the Church would oppose it.

In 1856, Alfred Russell Wallace developed a similar theory. A copy of Wallace's paper was sent to Darwin by a friend. This prompted Darwin to publish his own theory along with that of Wallace.

In the same year Darwin started working on a book which was to present his detailed theory on natural selection. This book, 'The Origin of Species' was published in November 1859.

Darwin explained that human beings were capable of creating a specific trait in a domesticated animal by carefully cross-breeding them for several generations. Horse breeders and pigeon breeders had been doing this for several centuries. This is known as artificial selection.

Darwin then asked, "If humans can artificially select species to go in a certain direction, is it not possible for Nature to do the same as well?"

Can Nature—meaning the surroundings—select certain species to survive and certain other species to become extinct?

Similarly, will this in turn allow certain variations within a certain species to thrive ahead of others in the same species?

Darwin found enough examples to support his theory. He called this process 'Natural Selection'.

Consider leaf-eating animals in an African forest. Several species of different heights co-exist. Suppose in one season the rains are poor. There will be fewer plants. Tall animal species will then have a natural advantage over those which are short as they can eat leaves which are higher up. Here, giraffes will be more successful than other grazing species.

Now, let us consider a single species. Some members of this species may be tall because of a 'tallness' gene. Others may be short because of a 'shortness' gene. During poor rains, the shorter members will find it difficult to get food and will die in large numbers. The taller members will survive. Because of their longevity, the taller members will give birth to more children, who in turn, will also be taller, since they inherit their traits from their parents. Over time, the taller members will increase within the population of this species.

Darwin proposed that only those species and individuals 'fit' to live in a given surrounding will survive. Here fitness does not necessarily mean strength, but ability to adjust to the surroundings.

Let us consider another example.

In a desert with light coloured sand, lives a desert rat species. This desert rat can appear in two colours—light and dark. Eagles prey on these rats. The eagle can easily to spot a dark coloured rat against the light coloured sand, but spotting the light coloured rat against a light background will be difficult.

Let us assume that the rat population starts with an equal number of light and dark coloured members. Over time, dark coloured rats will dwindle in number since eagles will find them easy prey. The light coloured rats will multiply in relatively large numbers.

Suddenly, because of a nearby volcanic eruption, the colour of the sand changes to dark. Now, the eagles will be able to spot the light coloured rats easily. Over the next several generations, the rat population will turn out to be mainly dark in colour.

Notice that the existing rats do not change their colour. The 'unlucky' coloured ones will vanish slowly, resulting in the lucky coloured rats increasing in numbers by way of reproduction.

Darwin stated in 'The Origin of Species':

"As many more individuals of each species are born than can possibly survive; and as, consequently, there is a frequently recurring struggle for existence, it follows that any being, if it vary however slightly in any manner profitable to itself, under the complex and sometimes varying conditions of life, will have a better chance of surviving, and thus be *naturally selected*. From the strong principle of inheritance, any selected variety will tend to propagate its new and modified form."

Is it possible for two species that look different today to have come about from the same forefathers? Can natural selection explain this possibility?

Though Mendel and Darwin were contemporaries, Darwin had not heard or read about Mendel's experiments with the pea plant. Darwin and Wallace arrived at their theories of natural selection and evolution independently, without a proper understanding of the genes.

Let us use genes to explain Darwin's thought process. Each particular species has a certain set of genes. During any copying process, some mistakes happen. When proteins are manufactured, a small copying error results in a different protein. The external chemical environment also causes some changes in a few genes here and there.

It has been observed that atomic radiation impacts genes and mutates or changes the genes. Children born in Nagasaki and Hiroshima where atom bombs were dropped, as well as in Chernobyl, where a nuclear power plant exploded, had malformed bodies with multiple fingers and limbs or missing body organs. This happened because the genetic coding was seriously affected by radiation.

Similarly, certain chemicals can seriously impact genetic makeup. This was observed in Bhopal, India, where there was a leak of Methyl Isocyanate gas from the Union Carbide plant. This killed several people, but also affected several fotuses genetically, resulting in malformed children. Thus, besides copying errors, the external environment can seriously impact genes.

Changes in genes are called mutations.

Any mutation in the gene structure results in a change in the look or behaviour of that member, from the rest of the species. This change may not offer any advantage to that member.

But what happens if the accidental change results in a crucial advantage to this member, allowing it to find more food or live a longer life or withstand diseases better than others? Then this member can use this advantage to produce more offspring. Since the offspring inherit the properties of the parent, the offspring will also carry this specific gene mutation.

However small the advantage, this advantage is multiplied severalfold over several generations. The result is a new species, slightly different from the original species.

Continuous gene mutation can then result in species which look very different from the original forefather species.

Thus, genetic variation and natural selection together contribute to the multiplicity of species. This is the core argument of Darwin. He named this process evolution.

Working backwards, it is possible to conclude that all life forms—plants, animals and microbes—might have developed from a small set of forefathers.

Darwin's theory says that all animals including human beings evolved from the same initial ancestral microbes, that all species are continuing to evolve. There could be more new species tomorrow, evolved from humans. They may possibly possess more powers than those of humans.

Can natural selection and evolution explain all the difficult questions we are asked? Let us take a look.

9. Can evolution explain everything?

Genes are the basic units defining the characteristics of a member of any species. Genes are contained in DNA. Genes have the ability to make copies of themselves. Genes together possess the formula to build a member of a species.

With this understanding, let us take up some interesting questions.

<u>Why are there males and females in several species?</u>

We have seen that most plants are hermaphrodites, i.e., the same plants produce male and female sex cells. In contrast most animals have distinct males and females.

Also, we have seen that two types of reproduction take place: asexual and sexual.

Which of the two types of reproduction is preferable?

We can say that evolution has favoured sexual reproduction. In this process shuffling of genes can take place. In asexual reproduction, the children are identical copies of the parents. If the parent has a defective gene, it is continually passed on.

In the case of sexual reproduction, better genes from the partner can help the offspring survive better.

Even in hermaphroditic plants, cross-pollination is preferred to self-pollination.

If a species starts with hermaphrodites, each member produces male and female cells. Slowly, through genetic variations, some members suppress their male part and act only as females. Through another genetic variation, some members behave more as males by suppressing their female part.

Over a particular period, male, female and hermaphrodite members will co-exist in that species. But over time, males and females will be preferred because of their role clarity. Males will excel in their male functionality and females will be likewise. Hermaphrodites will be left behind and will not be chosen as sexual partners by either males or females.

This will result in hermaphrodites slowly dying out as they cannot pass on their genes down the line.

This is the reason for the existence of distinct males and females in evolved animal species.

Are human beings the most evolved organisms?

In certain aspects, human beings are the most evolved, though in certain functions, animals have better features, depending on what will help the survival of a particular species in a particular environment.

In thinking capacity, humans are the best equipped. We have the best developed brain and central nervous system. The closest to humans are the apes. Humans evolved from the apes.

Humans are not the most advanced when it comes to muscle power. Elephants are stronger and bigger. Lions and tigers are fiercer than humans. Eagles have eyes much more powerful than human eyes.

Ants and insects have far better ability than humans to track the smell of chemicals. Dogs have better smelling capabilities. A bat has the ability to send out ultrasound signals and track objects even in darkness.

Birds have the ability to fly, which humans don't. Humans cannot swim like fish or whales.

So, it is only in one aspect—a highly evolved brain capable of thinking—that humans are ahead (by a long distance) of every known species on earth.

Are new species evolving every day?

Yes. However we have to understand the evolutionary time scales. Evolution does not happen over one or two years. Not even over a hundred or two hundred years. It happens over several thousand years. Thus, we are unlikely to see the evolution of any new species in our own lifetime.

We can see shorter evolution time cycles in microbial space. Several bacteria and viruses mutate faster than other complex species. Take for example the bird flu virus called H5N1. This virus has the ability to mutate faster and take a different form.

How are complex life forms formed from a simple life form?

A single-celled microbe is the simplest life form. Any multi-celled organism is a complex life form. Over stages, several systems have evolved within a complex life form to make its survival chances better.

Development of a digestive system is the most basic step. Since organisms were getting a variety of food, it was important for life forms to process the food and break them into a simple enough format they can use.

Subsequently, a blood circulation system was developed to carry nutrients and glucose to various parts of the body.

Since oxygen is required for burning glucose, a respiratory system was evolved, which extracts oxygen from air or water and supplies it to the blood stream.

Delivery of information to various parts of the body happens through two processes:

- Nervous system: neurons spread across the body and convey information through electrical and chemical processes.

- Different hormones are secreted to provide switching signals for certain actions.

The skeletal system was developed to provide stability to the body. Skin provides protection to the body from external attacks.

For mobility, a variety of systems have developed in several species.

Some species have a fairly well developed brain that controls the central nervous system. However, several primitive life forms do not have a brain. In these life forms, actions are pre-programmed and involuntary.

Each development—be it the brain or the eyes or the muscles or the wings—has happened over time and over several thousands of years. This can be interpreted by looking at the 'partially developed' organs in certain species.

Several organisms have no eyes. At the same time, several organisms have well developed eyes, with lenses and retina. Some animals have a socket in which some kind of liquid is secreted. This liquid droplet acts as a lens providing a low quality reflection of the surroundings.

Going from no-eye to a socket with oozing liquid is a great advance by itself. But from there, a solid expanding and contracting lens is a huge step. Two eyes at a specific distance to remove parallax error and offer a three-dimensional (3D) view is impressive evolution. The ability to understand different colours is another major evolutionary step.

In Nature, we can see all these types of eyes present now in several species. This has helped us to understand how the evolutionary process has worked across these species.

The heart has also evolved like this: a two-chambered heart (fish), a three-chambered heart (amphibians), something between three-chambered and four-chambered hearts (reptiles) and a four-chambered heart (birds and mammals including humans).

The brain has also evolved in this manner. Plants and several animals have nothing resembling a brain.

The brain is part of the central nervous system. A primitive central nervous system exists in worms (Annelida). They possess the basics of a brain-like organ.

From there on, more and more complex brains and central nervous systems have evolved in other animals.

Insects (Arthropoda) have small but nevertheless powerful brains. They can find prey, target and hunt them. Without a brain and the ability to recognise patterns, this is not possible. Those animals without brain just wait for a prey to touch them and then grab and swallow them.

Once we reach vertebrates, the brain size becomes larger and its functionality more complex. All mammals have very well developed brains, capable of image recognition and storage (memory). Human brains are the best developed.

Birds and mammals can think and act. They can communicate amongst members of their own family.

In primates (apes), the brain is large, while in humans, it is the largest so far. Complex thinking, verbal skills, development of languages, mathematics and tool building have been possible only because of the size of our brain.

Animals, other than humans, can think and convey their ideas primarily through their actions and the expression of their feelings (anger, aggression, sadness, fear). Only humans can express their feelings through written and spoken language.

10. Origin of life

We have now seen that multiple species have developed from a few simple species through evolution.

But how did life of any kind come about in the first place?

It is estimated that the universe was formed around 13.7 billion years ago. For a very long time after the formation of the universe, there was no life. Life was formed only around 4.4 billion years ago.

For life as we know it to form, the basic essentials are water and carbon.

Darwin wrote to a friend in 1871 that "Life may have begun in a warm little pond, with all sorts of ammonia and phosphoric salts, lights, heat, electricity, etc. present, so that a protein compound was chemically formed ready to undergo still more complex changes."

The only difficulty is that, our current atmosphere does not allow for such a reaction to take place. In the intense heat and pressure, any carbon compound formed will burn off to produce carbon dioxide.

However, 4.4 billion years ago, we wouldn't have had the kind of atmosphere that we have currently. That would have aided in the creation of an organic chemical compound as Darwin suggested. That compound must have had the capability to self-replicate. It might have created identical copies of itself from nearby material.

Instead of one, several self-replicating organic compounds might have formed. Each species thus created must have fought against others. Over time, they started building protein cell wall shields around them, and then created a nucleus with the DNA code and so on.

Slowly, the surrounding temperature and pressure started changing and the species also started evolving to form the kind of microbes we see even today.

Once single-celled organisms were formed, it is easy to imagine how multi-celled organisms could have come about from them through the process of Darwinian evolution.

If tomorrow, all life forms become extinct because of a nuclear war, life can still evolve on the earth in a manner similar to the evolution described above.

Since the 1950s, a number of experiments were proposed and conducted to replicate the condition of the earth a few billion years ago, to see whether a self-replicating life form can be created experimentally.

But no satisfactory experiments have taken place. This will be a hotly researched area over the next few decades.

Whatever the manner in which life originated, the theory of evolution holds good for explaining later developments.

11. Genetics and the future

Historically, humans have succeeded in cross-breeding animals and plants to achieve desired results - perhaps better tasting bananas or better looking pet dogs. This is, in essence, genetics.

With Mendel's theories on inheritance of characteristics from parents and subsequent understanding of DNA as the carrier of genes, a lot of research has taken place in the field of genetics.

One of the advances in genetic research is the creation of recombinant DNA. Researchers can cut portions of a DNA by applying certain chemicals on it. Using this process, they can cut relevant portions of DNA from several different members and stitch the pieces together to recreate a new DNA.

Instead of several generations of cross-breeding, through recombinant DNA, researchers can put together what they want within a few years or even months. Such a DNA can be put back in a cell, and this cell can be grown into a full organism.

This method has been applied to create genetically modified plant seeds. This has happened in both food crops such as maize and vegetables as well as utility crops like cotton. However, there is much resistance in using food from genetically modified grains or even using clothes made from genetically modified cotton.

Using similar genetic technology, some companies have created what are called 'Terminator seeds'. These seeds will grow into a plant, but will not produce seeds for the next sowing. The seeds of the grown up plant will be 'dead'. This will force farmers to keep buying seeds for every crop, from the manufacturer.

Cloning is another technology in which research has been substantial. Several animals have been cloned.

Natural cloning is not unusual! In fact, all asexual reproduction methods create identical clones of the parent, because both the parent and the children have identical genes. What we are talking about is artificial cloning.

A fertilised egg is taken and through a surgical process, the cell's DNA is removed. Instead, in its place, DNA from an animal which has to be cloned (source) is inserted. This replanted DNA cell is put back in a mother's womb to grow naturally.

The animal born from this process will look identical to the source animal from which DNA was taken. This is known as nuclear cloning. Though there were claims of nuclear cloning as early as 1952, the most well known and proven cloning happened in 1997. A sheep named Dolly was cloned at the Roslin Institute in Edinburgh, Scotland. This sheep lived for about six years. Since then several other animals have been cloned.

It is important to understand that cloning does not result in an identical replica of an existing person, as is normally shown in some science fiction movies. Instead, a new born baby is created which however looks like the source, when the source was born. They will have the same body features.

Life

There are several arguments for and against human cloning. There will be several debates in the future too on whether human cloning should be allowed or not.

There are some people who argue that cloning of extinct species should be allowed.

Most of you would have watched the movie Jurassic Park, where dinosaur DNA was used in a frog cell to recreate dinosaurs. Modern genetic research has shown that it is very much possible and this may happen in the future.

Life is not a mystery anymore.

We understand what happens in a plant and an animal. We understand what happens in our bodies. We understand how traits are inherited from our parents and how we pass on our traits to our offspring.

Though we still do not know for certain how life actually originated on earth, we do know some likely possibilities by which this might have happened. We have a fairly good idea of how complex life forms such as us humans have evolved from simple microbes.

We continue to search for life forms in other planets such as Mars and Venus. We continue our efforts to look for life elsewhere beyond our solar system.

Life is fascinating.

Medical research and advances in genetics can help in extending our lives by a few more years. But we also realise that there is no way we can live forever.

We however, will continue to live as long as small fragments of our DNA—the genes—are passed on to our offspring.

We are, thus, immortal. To be precise, our genes are immortal.

Provided, we make sure that our human race does not become extinct. For that, we need to make sure that animals and plants do not become extinct. Remember, every life form on earth depends on another for survival. And the urgent need of the hour is to preserve biodiversity.

———